W9-BNJ-600

ME TOO!

BY MERCER MAYER

HOUGHTON MIFFLIN COMPANY

BOSTON

ATLANTA   DALLAS   GENEVA, ILLINOIS   PALO ALTO   PRINCETON

Me Too! written and illustrated by Mercer Mayer. Copyright © 1983 by Mercer Mayer. Reprinted by permission of Western Publishing Company, Inc.

Houghton Mifflin Edition, 1996
Copyright © 1996 by Houghton Mifflin Company. All rights reserved.

Printed in the U.S.A.

ISBN: 0-395-75262-0

23456789-B-99 98 97 96 95

When my little sister saw
me riding my skateboard,
she said…

Me too!

Then I had to help her ride.

I had a paper airplane
that I made myself.
But my little sister
saw it and said…

Me too!

Then she threw it
in a tree.

I went hiking with my friends and
my little sister said, "Me too!"

I had to carry her because she got tired.

When my little sister
saw us playing football,
she said…

Me too!

Then we had to be too careful.

When the snow fell I got my sled and went to the top of the hill.

Guess what my little sister said.

I went skating on the pond.
My little sister said, "Me too!"
She doesn't know how to skate,
so I had to hold her up.

Me too!

There was one last piece of cake.
My little sister said…

I had to cut it in half,
even though I saw it first.

When I went fishing she said, "Me too!" Then she caught the biggest fish.

I went to my secret tree house. My little sister said...

Me too!

Mom said I had to help her up.

Everything I do
my little sister says,
"Me too!"

Today my little sister
had a candy cane of
her very own.

Guess what my little sister said.